JOHN MEI

DARK PEAK CHALLENGE WALK

by

JOHN N. MERRILL

Maps and Photographs

by John N. Merrill.

a J.N.M. PUBLICATION

1988

i

a J.N.M. PUBLICATION

JNM PUBLICATIONS,
WINSTER,
MATLOCK,
DERBYSHIRE.
DE4 2DQ

This book is copyright under the Berne Convention. All rights are reserved. Apart from any fair dealing for the purposes of private study, research, criticism or review, as permitted under the Copyright Act, 1956, no part of this publication may be reproduced, stored in a retrieval system, or transmitted in any other form by any means, electronic, electrical, chemical, mechanical, optical, phótocopying, recording or otherwise, without the prior permission of the copyright owner. Enquiries should be addressed to the publishers.

Conceived, edited, typeset, designed, marketed and distributed by John N. Merrill.

© Text and route — John N. Merrill 1988

© Maps and photographs — John N. Merrill 1988

First Published — September 1988

ISBN 0 907496 66 0

Meticulous research has been undertaken to ensure that this publication is highly accurate at the time of going to press. The publishers, however, cannot be held responsible for alterations, errors or omissions, but they would welcome notification of such for future editions.

Printed by The Amadeus Press Ltd, Huddersfield

Set in Futura — medium and bold.

ABOUT JOHN N. MERRILL

John combines the characteristics and strength of a mountain climber with the stamina and athletic capabilities of a marathon runner. In this respect he is unique and has to his credit a whole string of remarkable long walks. He is without question the world's leading marathon walker.

Over the last fifteen years he has walked more than 100,000 miles and successfully completed ten walks of at least 1,000 miles or more.

His six major walks in Great Britain are —
Hebridean Journey .... 1,003 miles
Northern Isles Journey... 913 miles
Irish Island Journey .... 1,578 miles
Parkland Journey.. 2,043 miles
Lands End to John o'Groats... 1,608 miles
and in 1978 he became the first person (permanent Guinness Book of Records entry) to walk the entire coastline of Britain — 6,824 miles in ten months.

In Europe he has walked across Austria — 712 miles — hiked the Tour of Mont Blanc, completed High Level Routes in the Dolomites, and the GR20 route across Corsica in training! In 1982 he walked across Europe — 2,806 miles in 107 days — crossing seven countries, the Swiss and French Alps and the complete Pyrennean chain — the hardest and longest mountain walk in Europe, with more than 600,000 feet of ascent!

In America he used the the world's longest footpath — The Appalachian Trail -2,200 miles — as a training walk. He has walked from Mexico to Canada via the Pacific Crest Trail in record time — 118 days for 2,700 miles. In Canada he has walked the Rideau Trail.

During the summer of 1984, John set off from Virginia Beach on the Atlantic coast, and walked 4,226 miles without a rest day, across the width of America to Santa Cruz and San Francisco on the Pacific Ocean. His walk is unquestionably his greatest achievement, being, in modern history, the longest, hardest crossing of the USA in the shortest time — under six months (178 days). The direct distance is 2,800 miles.

Between major walks John is out training in his own area — the Peak District National Park. As well as walking in other parts of Britain and Europe he has been trekking in the Himalayas five times. He has created more than ten challenge walks which have been used to raise more than £250,000 for charity. From his own walks he raised over £80,000. He is author of more than ninety books, most of which he publishes himself. His book sales are in excess of 2 million.

CONTENTS

INTRODUCTION

Many people who have walked some of my other day challenge walks frequently asked for another in the Peak District. I had already been thinking along these lines, for the other one is basically a "White Peak" challenge. The Dark Peak offers numerous permutations and for the last year I have pooling my thoughts as to a route. At first I wanted to do Kinder and Bleaklow but in reality the routes were too long and not really safe for the less experienced in bad weather. In the end I decided upon Hathersage as the start and finish, for it has all amenities including a Youth Hostel and campsite nearby.

With the start finalised I toyed with several route options before finalising this route. Unlike my other walks I decided to do it anti-clockwise, and for me I saw many of my favourite places from the other side, creating a walk which abounds in wide views all the way. I finalised the route on paper by Christmas but because of so many other books to complete it was five months before I could do my inaugural walk; and what a day I chose — mid May and continuous sun all day. I ended up very sunburnt and with two large blisters from my new boots, but a walk I will remember with great affection for years to come.

I left Hathersage car park at 9.30 a.m. and adopted a steady pace as I began the climb via North Lees Hall to the top of Stanage Edge. Incredibly there were few about and all day I saw hardly anyone — they didn't know what they were missing. My route took me over High Neb and down to Moscar. Here followed the next gentle but long ascent along the incomparable Derwent Edge past the Salt Cellar to Back Tor. Next came a long descent which in its latter stages is quite steep to the aptly named Walker's Clough and Derwent Reservoir. As I walked along Derwent Edge I could see the summit pinnacle of Win Hill, knowing this was my last peak of the day. To get there involved a short ascent and descent via Lockerbrook to the River Ashop. Here the final ascent began, steep at first but from Hope Cross more gentle as I walked the spine of Win Hill to its rocky crest. Standing on the summit the view took in the whole of the route. Footsore I descended to Thornhill and on past the incredibly attractive Bamford Mill into Bamford and the first shops and pubs on the walk! The final three miles were across the fields ascending and descending back to Hathersage.

I was sorry it was over — a fantastic walk with breathtaking views all the way. I can only hope that on your walk you enjoy such fine weather and see the beauty of this area at its best. Have a good walk and let me know how you get on.

HAPPY WALKING!

John N. Merrill.

JOHN N. MERRILL
Winster, Derbyshire. May 1988.

ABOUT THE WALK —

Whilst every care is taken detailing and describing the walk in this book, it should be borne in mind that the countryside changes by the seasons and the work of man. I have described the walk to the best of my ability, detailing what I have found on the walk in the way of stiles and signs. Obviously with the passage of time stiles become broken or replaced by a ladder stile or even a small gate. Signs too have a habit of being broken or pushed over. All the route follows rights of way and only on rare occasions will you have to overcome obstacles in its path, such as a barbed wire fence or electric fence.

The seasons bring occasional problems whilst out walking which should also be borne in mind. In the height of summer paths become overgrown and you will have to fight your way through in a few places. In low lying areas the fields are often full of crops, and although the pathline goes straight across it may be more practical to walk round the field edge to get to the next stile or gate. In summer the ground is generally dry but in autumn and winter, especially because of. our climate, the surface can be decidedly wet and slippery; sometimes even glutonous mud!

These comments are part of countryside walking which help to make your walk more interesting or briefly frustrating. Standing in a farmyard up to your ankles in mud might not be funny at the time but upon reflection was one of the highlights of the walk!

LADYBOWER VIADUCT FROM WIN HILL

ABOUT HATHERSAGE — Hathersage is extremely rich in local and national history. Many old buildings and industries remain. In the 19th century the village had a thriving needle manufacturing trade and several of the old works are still standing. Just behind the Hathersage Inn in Besom Lane is a three-storey high building built by the Furniss family in 1781 and used to manufacture buttons. In the churchyard is the grave to Little John, the faithful companion of Robin Hood. From a 29½ inch thigh bone taken from the grave, Little John would have been eight foot tall. The 14th century church contains several brasses to the Eyre family who once owned more than 20,000 acres in the area. North Lees Hall was built by the Eyre family as were several others in the surrounding area.

HOW TO DO IT -

ABBEY GRANGE PATH SIGN

The route is covered by the Ordance Survey maps —
1:25,000 Pathfinder Series — Sheet No SK 28/38 — Sheffield.
1:25,000 Outdoor Leisure Map — The Dark Peak.

The walk is devised to be done in a single day, allowing about 8 hours to complete the circuit. It is not a race but simply a hard high level route around some of the Peak District's finest scenery, to be enjoyed at your own individual pace. Most of the route is on well defined and used paths which in bright sunny weather are easy to follow. In rain and mist places like Derwent Edge need care. Where the route crosses roads, such as at Moscar and at Fairholmes, the walk can be aborted if needed. For those who complete the walk a special four-colour embroidered badge and signed certificate by John Merrill is available from JNM Publications. A master record of all those who walk the route is also maintained by them.

The whole route has been carefully mapped, and you should have no difficulty in finding your way round in good weather. You should always carry the 1:25,000 O.S. maps and be well versed in how to use a compass. Whilst the route follows well defined paths it is advisable in misty weather to use your compass to ensure you are walking in the right direction.

From Hathersage you gradually ascend to Stanage Edge but don't rush for you have a long way to go and a lot of ascending to do! The secret to completing the route is to adopt a steady pace and maintain it all day. From Stanage it is level walking before descending to Moscar. Here you ascend gently but for a long time along Derwent Edge to the summit of Back Tor. Here you descend gently at first but steeply later to Derwent Reservoir. A short ascent from Fairholmes takes you to Lockerbrook and the descent to the River Ashop. Here the final but long ascent begins to the summit of Win Hill. Then you descend to Bamford and follow undulating paths back to Hathersage.

The route is a committing one with very few facilities until the final stages, so carry suffcient food and liquid for the day. Back-up parties can meet you at Moscar and Fairholmes. The latter has toilets and refreshments in the summer. Once you leave here, apart from crossing the A57 road you are committed to ascend Win Hill before descending to Bamford where there are shops and pubs. Hathersage 3 miles later has everything; even a railway station! As a rough guide it is 3 hours walk from Hathersage to Back Tor and a further 3 hours from there to the summit of Win Hill. 2 hours from there you should be in Hathersage!

HATHERSAGE TO STANAGE EDGE – 2½ MILES

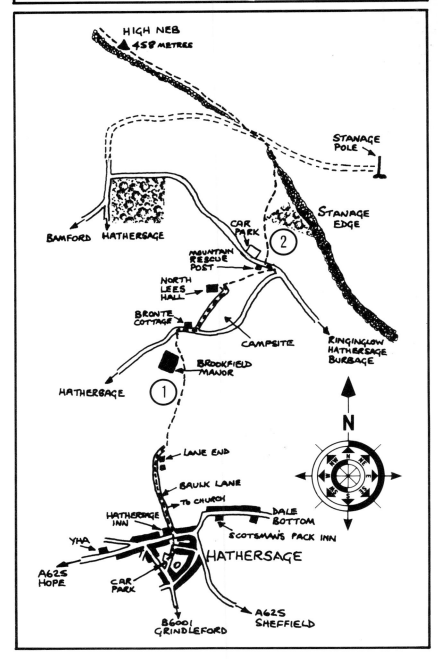

HIGH NEB
▲ 458 METRES

STANAGE POLE

STANAGE EDGE

CAR PARK

②

BAMFORD HATHERSAGE

MOUNTAIN RESCUE POST

NORTH LEES HALL

BRONTE COTTAGE

CAMPSITE

RINGINGLOW HATHERSAGE BURBAGE

BROOKFIELD MANOR

HATHERSAGE

①

N

LANE END

BAULK LANE

TO CHURCH

HATHERSAGE INN

DALE BOTTOM

SCOTSMAN'S PACK INN

YHA

HATHERSAGE

A625 HOPE

CAR PARK

A625 SHEFFIELD

B6001 GRINDLEFORD

HATHERSAGE TO STANAGE EDGE — 2½ MILES

900 feet of ascent — allow 1 hour.

MAP — O.S. 1:25,000 Pathfinder Series — Sheet No SK 28/38 — Sheffield.

CAR PARK — Oddfellows Lane, Hathersage — opposite swimming pool.

ABOUT THE SECTION — A steady ascent from the village first along a track then path past the impressive North Lees Hall to the top of Stanage Edge. The edge is the longest in the Peak District — 4 miles — and is a popular climbing ground with more than 600 routes of varying difficulties.

WALKING INSTRUCTIONS — Turn left out of the car park along Oddfellows Lane. Where it turns sharp right keep straight ahed to the stile and path to reach another stile and the A625 road. Cross to your right to the righthand side of the Hathersage Inn and walk along Baulk Lane. You keep on this track for the next ¾ mile. Soon you pass the cricket field on your left which you walk past at the end of the walk. Keep on the track past the houses Derwent Holme and Lane End. At the latter the track turns right then left. Pass through three gates or stiles and just after the third one, leave the track as footpath signed and follow the path to a stile on the righthand side of the buildings of Brookfield Manor. Follow the path past it and round to your right to a gate and Birley Lane.

Turn right and pass Bronte Cottage on your left, and shortly afterwards turn left up the drive to North Lees Hall. Just ahead is North Lees Campsite. Walk up the drive, and just past the Hall bear right and follow the ascending grass track to a stile and trees and on to the road beneath Stanage Edge. Turn left, and a few yards later right, and follow the distinct diagonally ascending path to your left up the slope towards the edge. The path is made of gritstone slabs — don't bear right in the woodland but keep ahead on the gently ascending path and gain the crest of the edge.

NORTH LEES HALL — Elizabethan turreted building built by the Eyre family in about 1594. The nearby Moorseats Hall has Bronte connections for Charlotte Bronte stayed here, resulting in her famous novel, Jane Eyre. In the book Moorseats is known as Moor House and North Lees Hall is described as Marsh End.

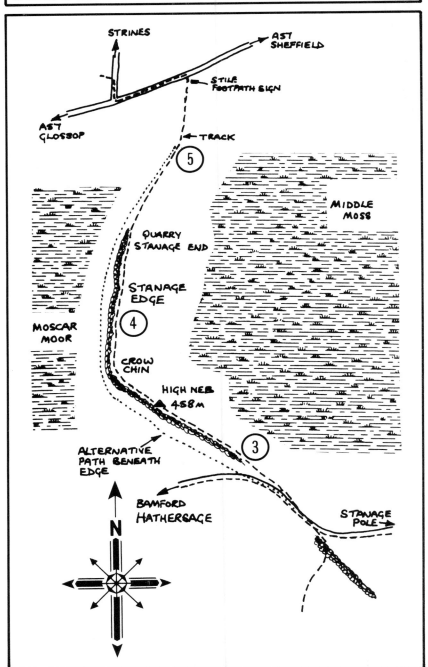

STRINES

A57
SHEFFIELD

STILE
FOOTPATH SIGN

A57
GLOSSOP

← TRACK

⑤

MIDDLE
MOSS

QUARRY
STANAGE END

STANAGE
EDGE

④

MOSCAR
MOOR

CROW
CHIN

HIGH NEB
▲ 458M

ALTERNATIVE
PATH BENEATH
EDGE

③

BAMFORD
HATHERSAGE

STANAGE
POLE →

N

STANAGE EDGE TO MOSCAR — 3 MILES

- 150 feet of ascent — allow 1¼ hours

MAP — O.S. 1:25,000 Pathfinder Series Sheet SK 28/38 — Sheffield.

ABOUT THE SECTION — High level walk along the top of Stanage Edge past the trig point — 458 metres on High Neb. A mile later you descend to the A57 road at Moscar.

WALKING INSTRUCTIONS — From the crest of the edge turn left along the path and gain the track to Stanage Pole. Bear left slightly down this to gain another path which keeps to the summit edge — you can also follow the path beneath the edge, gained lower down the track; both join up later. Continue along the edge to the trig point and a mile later the remnants of a small quarry at Stanage End. Continue along the top and in ½ mile you descend to the path beneath the edge and continue ahead descending, now along a track to a stile and footpath sign before the A57 road at Moscar. There is a small car parking space here. Turn left down the A57 road.

VIEW TOWARDS HIGH NEB, STANAGE EDGE

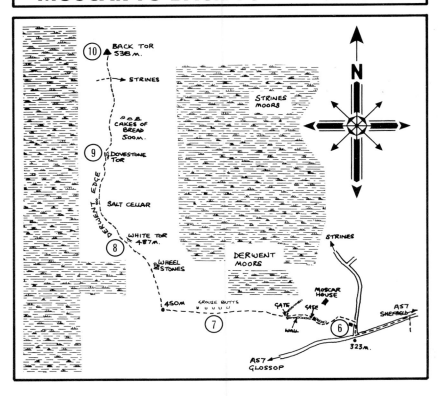

MOSCAR PATH SIGN

MOSCAR TO BACK TOR — 4½ MILES

- 750 feet of ascent — allow 1¾ hours.

MAPS — O.S. 1:25,000 Pathfinder Series — Sheet No SK 28/38 — Sheffield.
- O.S. 1:25,000 Outdoor Leisure Series — The Dark Peak.

ABOUT THE SECTION — The ascent onto Derwent Edge with its magnificent views over Kinder, Bleaklow and the Derwent Valley. The ascent culminates in the summit of Back Tor. En route passing the impressive gritstone formations of the "Wheel Stones", "Salt Cellar" and "Cakes of Bread". A section to savour.

WALKING INSTRUCTIONS — From the A57 road turn left down it and in just over¼ mile, turn right onto the Strines Road — alas the Strines Inn is a good two miles away! A few yards along the road turn left at the footpath sign — Derwent — and walk past the solitary house on its right along a track. 50 yards or so past the house, as footpath signed, leave the track on your left and follow the curving path across a stream to a gate and footpath sign — Via Derwent Edge to Derwent. Go straight across and soon swing left as you follow a good path and begin the ascent to Derwent Edge passing several grouse butts.

Little over a mile later on the summit of the edge beside a path sign — Moscar/Derwent — turn right and continue ascending gently on a wide path. First pass the Wheel Stones, then White Tor, the Salt Cellar — a little to your left — and on past Dovestone Tor and the Cakes of Bread. Little over¼ mile later reach Bradfield Gate Head and path sign — Strines/Abbey Grange. You turn left here and follow the Abbey Grange path, but first you must continue ahead to the summit of Back Tor!

WHEEL STONES

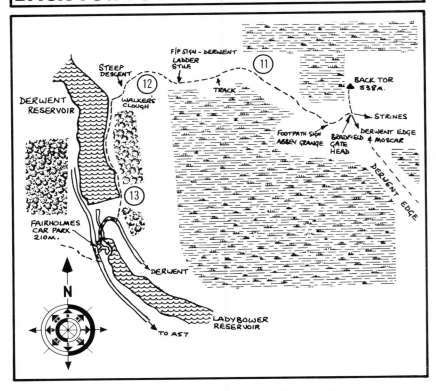

THE SALT CELLAR

BACK TOR TO FAIRHOLMES CAR PARK — 3½ MILES

- 1,050 feet of descent — allow 1½ hours.

MAP — O.S. 1:25,000 Outdoor Leisure Series — The Dark Peak.

ABOUT THE SECTION — A gradual descent across moorland at first for two miles. Followed by a steep descent but with impressive views of Derwent Reservoir as you gain Walker's Clough. A short level section brings you to the Derwent Dam wall with a final descent to Fairholmes.

WALKING INSTRUCTIONS — Retrace your steps back to Bradfield Gate Head and its footpath sign, from Back Tor. Turn right and descend on the path which soon swings right at a footpath sign — Abbey Grange. Keep on the path for the next mile and in ¾ mile it bears left and ¼ mile later joins a track. ¼ mile later gain a ladder stile and footpath sign — Derwent Reservoir. The path bears right and in ¼ mile reaches another sign. Less than a further ¼ mile you reach another sign and the steep descent to Walker's Clough. Turn right for a few yards then left on the descending path, and at the bottom reach the gate and woodland of Walker's Clough. Descend the track to the track above Derwent Reservoir. Turn left along the track and in ¾ mile ascend the wooden stile on your right beside the dam wall. Follow the path — not the steep one — and descend through the trees to the road. Turn right and follow it round to your right to the road junction ¼ mile away. On your left is Fairholmes picnic site and car park.

BACK TOR SUMMIT

FAIRHOLMES TO HAGGWATER BRIDGE — 2 MILES

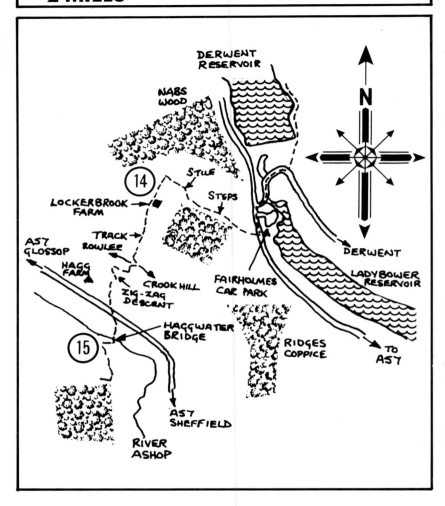

DERWENT RESERVOIR — was built in 1916 and has a holding capacity of 2,120 million gallons. The dam wall is 178 feet thick at its base tapering to 10 feet at the top. The wall is 114 feet high and 1,110 feet long. Ladybower Reservoir was started in 1935 and completed ten years later and has a holding capacity of 6,300 million gallons. The average annual rainfall for the area is 54 inches.

FAIRHOLMES TO HAGGWATER BRIDGE (RIVER ASHOP) — 2 MILES

- 500 feet of ascent — allow 50 minutes.

MAP — O.S. 1:25,000 Outdoor Leisure Series — The Dark Peak.

ABOUT THE SECTION — First you ascend through pine trees to Lockerbrook before descending past Hagg Farm to the A57 road and River Ashop. Here the last major ascent begins!

WALKING INSTRUCTIONS — At the road junction on the right of Fairholmes car park, turn left along the road and in about 80 yards turn right at the Concessionary Footpath, signed Lockerbrook and Old Railway. First you follow an ascending track and after crossing a water channel ascend wooden steps in the pine trees and follow the switchback path eventually reaching a stile and open fields. Ascend the field to a track and turn left along it past Lockerbrook Farm to a cross roads of track. Keep ahead and descend the switch back track into woodland and eventually pass the entrance to Hagg Farm. Just afterwards cross the A57 to a gate and bridlepath sign — Hope and Edale. Continue descending on a track to the River Ashop and Haggwater Bridge.

DESCENDING TO DERWENT RESERVOIR

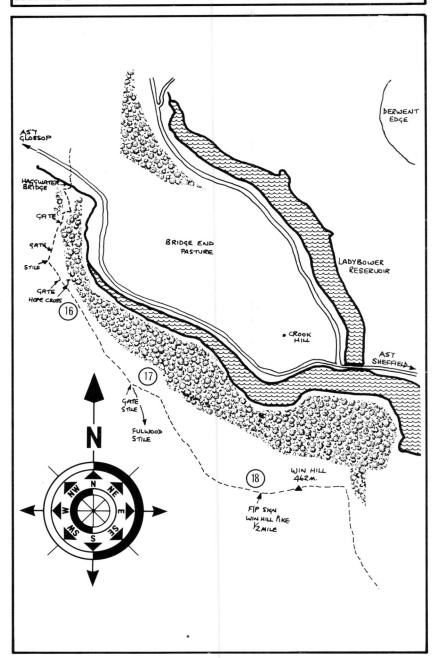

ASY
GLOSSOP

HAGGWATER
BRIDGE

GATE

GATE

STILE

GATE
HOPE CROSS

(16)

(17)

GATE
STILE

FULWOOD
STILE

DERWENT
EDGE

BRIDGE END
PASTURE

LADYBOWER
RESERVOIR

CROOK
HILL

AST
SHEFFIELD

(18)

WIN HILL
462M.

F/P SIGN
WIN HILL PIKE
½ MILE

N

NW N NE

W   E

SW S SE

HAGGWATER BRIDGE (RIVER ASHOP) TO WIN HILL — 3 MILES

- 800 feet of ascent — allow 1½ hours.

MAP — O.S. 1:25,000 Outdoor Leisure Series — The Dark Peak.

ABOUT THE SECTION — The final major ascent of the walk. The steepest part is first as you ascend through pine trees to Hope Cross. From here on the spine of Win Hill you gradually ascend to the rocky summit more than two miles away. All the time the views are spectacular along the Edale Valley; over Ladybower Reservoir; to the Hope Valley and Lose Hill and ridge to Mam Tor.

WALKING INSTRUCTIONS — After Haggwater Bridge turn right onto the track in the pine trees and begin the ascent. In a few yards it turns left and in less than a¼ mile you reach another track. Turn right along it, still ascending, and this too turns left and eventually reaches a gate and open fields. Continue ascending with the woodland on your left to another gate. Just after this reach a cross-roads of paths. Turn left and ascend the stile following the signposted path — Fulwood Stile Lane 1¼ miles. In less than¼ mile reach Hope Cross. Continue on the path/track and in¾ mile reach a stile and gate. Just after the track begins descending to Fulwood Stile Lane. Here turn left on a path and begin following the well defined path to the summit of Win Hill 1½ miles away.

WIN HILL'S ROCKY SUMMIT

15

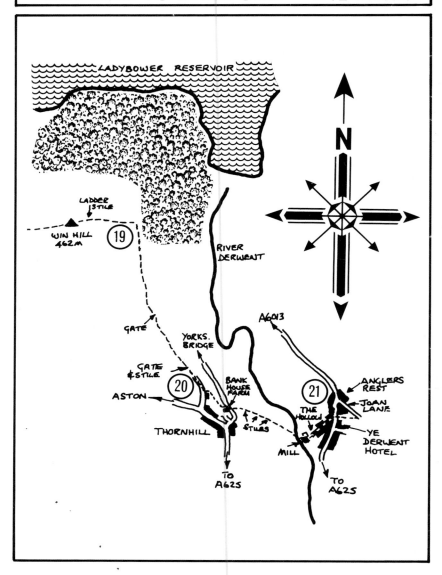

BAMFORD MILL — is on the site of a corn mill. In 1782 Christopher Kirk, a local farmer and miller, used it as a cotton mill. A bad fire destroyed the building in 1791 and the present building was built soon afterwards harnessing the River Derwent to drive spinning frames. In the 19th century a beam engine was installed and in 1907 a steam engine was operating.

WIN HILL TO BAMFORD — 2½ MILES

- 1,100 feet of descent — allow 1 hour.

**MAPS — O.S. 1:25,000 Outdoor Leisure Series — The Dark Peak.
- O.S. 1:25,000 Pathfinder Series — Sheet No SK 28/38 —
Sheffield.**

ABOUT THE SECTION — The long descent to civilisation! A bit hard on the muscles after the route so far but the worst is over and you are into the home straight! You descend to Thornhill then across the fields to Bamford and its impressive mill beside the River Derwent. Bamford has shops and pubs to fortify yourself before the final miles back to Hathersage.

WALKING INSTRUCTIONS — From the summit continue along the ridge and descend to the ladder stile. Cross this and ignore the grass path on right and continue straight ahead descending through sparse woodland to the perimeter fence of the forest. Turn right on a good path and follow this close to a wall on your right for a little over ¼ mile. Keep left and descend more steeply on the path/track for ¼ mile. Here the track curves right; leave it and descend to your left to a small gate and path. Continue descending to another gate. Continue straight ahead to another stile and gate as you now walk down a walled track to the first house of Thornhill. Leave the track on the lefthand side of the house at a stile and follow the narrow path round to your right with the field boundary on your right. After about 80 yards the path forks, take the lefthand branch and continue descending to a stile on the edge of Bank House Farm. Turn left to the road and turn right.

Walk past the house on your right, and just past a lane on your left is a stile. Go through this and descend to another and cross the remains of a railway line. Over the next stile bear right past a barn to another stile. The path is ill-defined but well stiled as you aim for Bamford Mill. At the River Derwent cross the footbridge opposite the mill and walk around its lefthand side to the lane — The Hollow. Turn left up this and in ¼ mile reach central Bamford. The shops are to your right and Ye Derwent Hotel can be seen. The route continue straight ahead.

ASHOPTON VIADUCT FROM WIN HILL

17

BAMFORD TO HATHERSAGE — 3 MILES

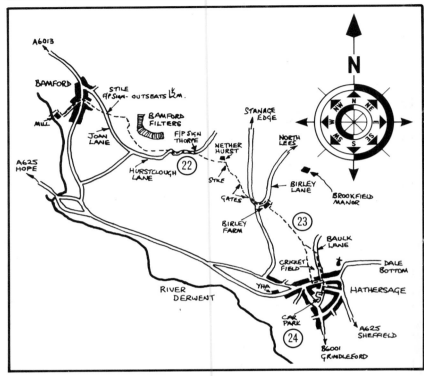

BAMFORD MILL

BAMFORD TO HATHERSAGE — 3 MILES

- 250 feet of ascent — allow 1 hour.

MAP — O.S. 1;25,000 Pathfinder Series Sheet No SK 28/38 — Sheffield.

ABOUT THE SECTION — The final miles crossing undulating countryside on little used rights of way, passing the Bamford Filters to gain Birley Lane. Here you descend for the last time to the Hood Brook and walk past the cricket field back into Hathersage.

WALKING INSTRUCTIONS — Cross the road opposite The Hollow to the footpath sign — Outseats 2 miles. Walk along the fenced path between the houses, then past the houses on a well stiled path. In 1/4 mile reach Joan Lane. Go straight across to a stile and another path sign — Outseats 1 1/2 miles. The path descends and ascends and just past the start of the wood you turn right into it and ascend to kissing gate and a tarmaced road. Turn right as signposted and in a few yards left, as signposted walking around the perimeter fence of the Bamford Filters. At the road entrance to the plant keep to the right of it to continue near the boundary fence to eventually descend along a fenced path and cross Upper Hurst Brook to gain Hurstclough Lane. Turn left and ascend this sunken lane for a little over 1/4 mile. Where it turns left, and now almost level, keep straight ahead on a fenced path — signposted Thorpe. In less than 1/4 mile reach Nether Hurst Farm. Walk along the track on the right of it. The bridleway is well signed here and where the farm road turns right keep ahead to the stile and bridleway sign. The path is ill-defined but you descend the field to your right with the hedge on your right. Cross a small stream and ascend with the hedge on your right. Although there is a track on your right at the top don't use it but continue ahead to a small gate. Ascend the next field diagonally to your right and in its top righthand corner is a gate and footpath sign before the road.

Turn right down the road to a T junction and turn left along Birley Lane. In a few yards pass Birley Farm on your right and at the farm gates is a stile. Go through this and then around the buildings in a clockwise direction to reach the next stile. Now begin your final descent, first with the field boundary on your right to the next stile. Over this continue descending to your right through the trees of Cliff Wood and cross the drive to Brookfield Manor and reach a footbridge over Hood Brook. Turn right along the path and in a few yards you can decide whether you cross the field to Baulk Lane and retrace your steps back to the car park. Alternatively if you walk beside the brook you walk along the edge of the cricket field and past the houses into Hathersage and the A625 road. Shops and cafes are on your right. To your left is the Hathersage Inn and the path back to the car park. The Youth Hostel is down the road past the George Hotel.

LOG

AVS 8do 21/10/90.
- Hard but enjoyable

DATE ...21/10/90... TIME STARTED ...10-30 am... TIME COMPLETED ...7.00 pm...

ROUTE POINT	MILE NO	TIME Arr	TIME Dep	COMMENTS/ WEATHER
HATHERSAGE	0		10.30	OVERCAST
BROOKFIELD MANOR	1			PASSED RAMBLING
NORTH LEES HALL	1½			GROUPS
STANAGE EDGE	2½			
HIGH NEB	3½		11-30	ISH
MOSCAR	5½			
WHITE TOR	8			WINDY + RAIN PUT WATERPROOFS
DOVESTONE TOR	9			ON - GOOD VIEWS OF DERWENT
BACK TOR	10		1.30	CLEARED UP BUT WINDY.
DERWENT RESERVOIR	12½			WENT TO UPPER DAM · LOST TIME,
FAIRHOLMES	13½			WHEELCHAIR EVENT WATER LEVELS V. LOW.
LOCKERBROOK	14			NEW FOREST TRACK CUT PATH - BUT REFOUND
HAGGWATER BRIDGE	15			SLUSHY
HOPE CROSS	16			GOOD VIEWS
WIN HILL SUMMIT	18½		5.00 pm	WINDY LIGHT FADING
THORNHILL	20			OVER FIELDS TO
BAMFORD	21			MILL. UP THE HOLLOW + ACROSS TO JOAN LANE
BAMFORD FILTERS	22			WOODY PATH DIFFICULT
BIRLEY LANE	22½			NEW HOUSING - ROUTE OK.
CRICKET FIELD	23½			FOUND BRIDGE OVER STREAM! -
HATHERSAGE	24		7.00	IN DARKNESS

AMENITIES GUIDE —

VILLAGE/ LOCATION	B & B	YHA	CAMP	INN	CAFE	SHOP	P.O.	CAR PARK
HATHERSAGE	●	●		●	●	●	●	●
NORTH LEES			●					
MOSCAR								●
FAIRHOLMES			●		●			●
BAMFORD	●			●	●	●		

INNS —

HATHERSAGE — Hathersage Inn
Little John Inn
Scotsman's Pack Inn

MOSCAR — Strines Inn — 2 miles from route.

BAMFORD — Angler's Rest
Ye Derwent Hotel

Y.H.A.

HATHERSAGE — Castleton Road, Hathersage, Sheffield. S30 1AH
Tel. 0433 — 50493

HAGG FARM — Hagg Farm, Snake Road, Bamford, Sheffield. S30 2BJ
Tel. 0433 — 51594

CAMPSITES

NORTH LEES — North Lees Campsite, Birley Lane.
Grid Ref: SK 235832.
Tel. Hope Valley 0433 — 20838

BED AND BREAKFAST — a random selection.

HATHERSAGE — Hathersage Inn — as above.

 Mrs M. Anderson, Hill Rise, Castleton Road,
Hathersage.
Tel. 0433 — 50318

Mrs B. Cross, Copperfield, Back Lane, Hathersage.
Tel. 0433 — 50277

TRAIL PROFILE — 3,300 FEET OF ASCENT

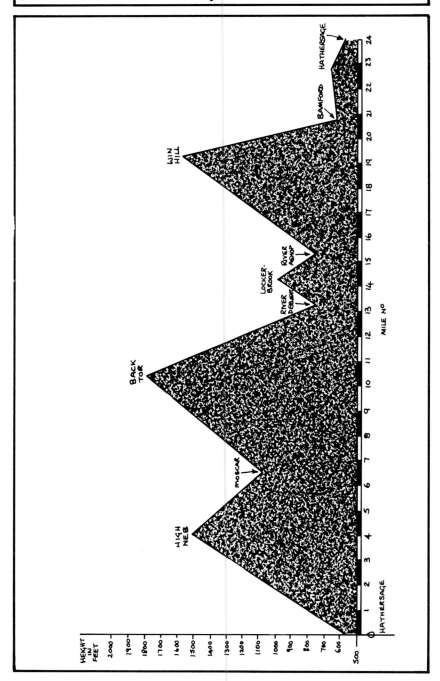

J M'S PEAK CHALLENGE

Badges are brown cloth with figure embroidered in four colours and measure — 3" wide x 3½" high.

BADGE ORDER FORM

Date completed ....

Time ....

NAME ....

ADDRESS ....

....

Price: £2.00 each including postage, VAT and signed completion certificate.

From: J.N.M. Publications, Winster, Matlock, Derbyshire, DE4 2DQ
Tel: Winster (062988) 454 — 24hr answering service.

********* **You may photocopy this form if needed** ********

THE JOHN MERRILL WALK BADGE — walk this route twice or complete another John Merrill's challenge walk and send details and cheque/PO for £2.00 for a special circular walk badge. Price includes postage and VAT.

EQUIPMENT NOTES — some personal thoughts

BOOTS — preferably with a full leather upper, of medium weight, with a vibram sole. I always add a foam cushioned insole to help cushion the base of my feet.

SOCKS — I generally wear two thick pairs as this helps minimise blisters. The inner pair are of loop stitch variety and approximately 80% wool. The outer are a thick rib pair of approximately 80% wool.

WATERPROOFS — for general walking I wear a T shirt or shirt with a cotton wind jacket on top. You generate heat as you walk and I prefer to layer my clothes to avoid getting too hot. Depending on the season will dictate how many layers you wear. In soft rain I just use my wind jacket for I know it quickly dries out. In heavy downpours I slip on a neoprene lined cagoule, and although hot and clammy it does keep me reasonably dry. Only in extreme conditions will I don overtrousers, much preferring to get wet and feel comfortable.

FOOD — as I walk I carry bars of chocolate, for they provide instant energy and are light to carry. In winter a flask of hot coffee is welcome. I never carry water and find no hardship from doing so, but this is a personal matter! From experience I find the more I drink the more I want and sweat. You should always carry some extra food such as Kendal mint cake, for emergencies.

RUCKSACKS — for day walking I use a climbing rucksac of about 40 litre capacity and although it leaves excess space it does mean that the sac is well padded, with an internal frame and padded shoulder straps. Inside apart from the basics for the day I carry gloves, balaclava, spare pullover and a pair of socks.

MAP & COMPASS — when I am walking I always have the relevant map — preferably the 1:25,000 scale — open in my hand. This enables me to constantly check that I am walking the right way. In case of bad weather I carry a compass, which once mastered gives you complete confidence in thick cloud or mist.

When in the Peak District why not visit Jarvis Books and look through their large stock of secondhand Mountain books.

They also have a superb selection of NEW Mountaineering, Walking Books and Guides to most parts of the world — and of course John Merrill's books.

Shop open — Monday to Saturday, 9.30 — 5.30

Jarvis Books, 57, Smedley Street East, Matlock, Derbyshire. DE4 3FQ
Tel. 0629 — 55322

Books Bought and Sold in ALL SUBJECTS "Mountain" catalogues issued.

REMEMBER AND OBSERVE THE COUNTRY CODE

Enjoy the countryside and respect its life and work.

Guard against all risk of fire.

Fasten all gates.

Keep your dogs under close control.

Keep to public paths across farmland.

Use gates and stiles to cross fences, hedges and walls.

Leave livestock, crops and machinery alone.

Take your litter home — pack it in, pack it out.

Help to keep all water clean.

Protect wildlife, plants and trees.

Take special care on country roads.

Make no unnecessary noise.

THE HIKER'S CODE

* Hike only along marked routes — do not leave the trail.

* Use stiles to climb fences; close gates.

* Camp only in designated campsites.

* Carry a light-weight stove.

* Leave the Trail cleaner than you found it.

* Leave flowers and plants for others to enjoy.

* Keep dogs on a leash.

* Protect and do not disturb wildlife.

* Use the trail at your own risk.

* Leave only your thanks — take nothing but photographs.

OTHER CHALLENGE WALKS BY JOHN N. MERRILL —

DAY CHALLENGES —

John Merrill's White Peak Challenge Walk — 25 miles.
Circular walk from Bakewell involving 3,600 feet of ascent.

John Merrill"s Yorkshire Dales Challenge Walk — 23 miles.
Circular walk from Kettlewell involving 3,600 feet of ascent.

John Merrill's North Yorkshire Moors Challenge Walk — 24 miles.
Circular walk from Goathland — a seaside bash — involving 2,000 feet of ascent.

The Little John Challenge Walk — 28 miles.
Circular walk from Edwinstowe in Sherwood Forest — Robin Hood country.

Peak District End to End Walks.
1. Gritstone Edge Walk — 23 miles down the eastern edge system.
2. Limestone Dale Walk — 24 miles down the limestone dales from Buxton to Ashbourne.

John Merrill's Staffordshire Moorlands Challenge Walk — 24 miles.
Circular walk from Oakamoor, taking in the finest scenery around the Churnet Valley.

Forthcoming titles —

John Merrill's Snowdonia Challenge Walk

Rutland Water Challenge Walk.

MULTIPLE DAY CHALLENGE WALKS —

The Limey Way — 40 miles
Down twenty limestone dales from Castleton to Thorpe in the Peak District.

The Peakland Way — 100 miles.
John Merrill's classic walk around the Peak District.

The River's Way — 43 miles.
Down the five main river systems of the Peak District, from Edale, the end of the Pennine Way, to Ilam.

Peak District High Level Route — 90 miles
Circular walk from Matlock taking in the highest and remotest parts of the Peak District.

Isle of Wight Coast Path — 80 miles.
Circular walk around the island passing stunning scenery — downs, heathland and magnificent cliffs.

OTHER BOOKS BY JOHN N. MERRILL PUBLISHED BY JNM PUBLICATIONS

DAY WALK GUIDES —

SHORT CIRCULAR WALKS IN THE PEAK DISTRICT
LONG CIRCULAR WALKS IN THE PEAK DISTRICT
CIRCULAR WALKS IN WESTERN PEAKLAND
SHORT CIRCULAR WALKS IN THE STAFFORDSHIRE MOORLANDS
SHORT CIRCULAR WALKS AROUND THE TOWNS AND VILLAGES OF THE PEAK DISTRICT
SHORT CIRCULAR WALKS AROUND MATLOCK
SHORT CIRCULAR WALKS IN THE DUKERIES
SHORT CIRCULAR WALKS IN SOUTH YORKSHIRE
SHORT CIRCULAR WALKS AROUND DERBY
SHORT CIRCULAR WALKS AROUND BAKEWELL
SHORT CIRCULAR WALKS AROUND BUXTON
SHORT CIRCULAR WALKS AROUND NOTTINGHAMSHIRE
SHORT CIRCULAR WALKS ON THE NORTHERN MOORS
40 SHORT CIRCULAR PEAK DISTRICT WALKS
SHORT CIRCULAR WALKS IN THE HOPE VALLEY

INSTRUCTION & RECORD —

HIKE TO BE FIT .... STROLLING WITH JOHN
THE JOHN MERRILL WALK RECORD BOOK

CANAL WALK GUIDES —

VOL ONE — DERBYSHIRE AND NOTTINGHAMSHIRE
VOL TWO — CHESHIRE AND STAFFORDSHIRE
VOL THREE — STAFFORDSHIRE
VOL FOUR — THE CHESHIRE RING
VOL FIVE — LINCOLNSHIRE & NOTTINGHAMSHIRE
VOL SIX — SOUTH YORKSHIRE
VOL SEVEN — THE TRENT & MERSEY CANAL

DAY CHALLENGE WALKS —

JOHN MERRILL'S WHITE PEAK CHALLENGE WALK
JOHN MERRILL'S YORKSHIRE DALES CHALLENGE WALK
JOHN MERRILL'S NORTH YORKSHIRE MOORS CHALLENGE WALK
PEAK DISTRICT END TO END WALKS
THE LITTLE JOHN CHALLENGE WALK
JOHN MERRILL'S LAKELAND CHALLENGE WALK
JOHN MERRILL'S STAFFORDSHIRE MOORLAND CHALLENGE WALK

MULTIPLE DAY WALKS -

THE RIVERS' WAY
PEAK DISTRICT HIGH LEVEL ROUTE
PEAK DISTRICT MARATHONS
THE LIMEY WAY
THE PEAKLAND WAY

COAST WALKS —

ISLE OF WIGHT COAST WALK
PEMBROKESHIRE COAST PATH
THE CLEVELAND WAY

HISTORICAL GUIDES —

DERBYSHIRE INNS
HALLS AND CASTLES OF THE PEAK DISTRICT & DERBYSHIRE
TOURING THE PEAK DISTRICT AND DERBYSHIRE BY CAR
DERBYSHIRE FOLKLORE
LOST INDUSTRIES OF DERBYSHIRE
PUNISHMENT IN DERBYSHIRE
CUSTOMS OF THE PEAK DISTRICT AND DERBYSHIRE
WINSTER — A VISITOR'S GUIDE
ARKWRIGHT OF CROMFORD
TALES FROM THE MINES by GEOFFREY CARR
PEAK DISTRICT PLACE NAMES by MARTIN SPRAY

JOHN'S MARATHON WALKS —

TURN RIGHT AT LAND'S END
WITH MUSTARD ON MY BACK
TURN RIGHT AT DEATH VALLEY
EMERALD COAST WALK

COLOUR GUIDES —

THE PEAK DISTRICT...Something to remember her by.

SKETCH BOOKS — by John Creber

NORTH STAFFORDSHIRE SKETCHBOOK